THE FACEBOOK JOB-SEEKER

7 TIPS TO CREATE A SUCCESSFUL FACEBOOK BRAND FOR YOUR DREAM JOB

Tejas Subrahmanya and Shubham Vatsyayan

Tejas Publishers

© *2016*

Disclaimer

The information provided in this book is designed to provide helpful information on the subjects discussed. The publisher and author are not responsible and liable for any damages or negative consequences from any action, to any person reading or following the information provided in this book. This book has been written to provide guidelines on the topic of reference, and not to be construed as the absolute truth. Readers are advised to exercise their discretion while applying the concepts descried in the book. References are provided for informational purposes only and do not constitute endorsement of any websites or other sources. Readers should be aware that the website listed in this book may change.

Copyright© 2016 Tejas Publishers

All rights reserved. No part of this publication may be reproduced, distributed, or transmitted in any form or by any means, including photocopying, recording, or other electronic or mechanical methods, without the prior written permission of the publisher, except in the case of brief quotations embodied in critical reviews and certain other non-commercial uses permitted by copyright law.

While attempts have been made to verify that the information contained in this publication is accurate, neither the author nor the publisher assumes any responsibility for errors, omissions, interpretations or usage of the subject matters herein.

This publication contains the opinions and ideas of its author and is intended for informational purposes only. The author and publisher shall in no event be held liable for any loss or other damages incurred during the usage of the publication.

Acknowledgement

This book is an effort to indicate that there is much more to Facebook that what meets the eye. Facebook is banned in universities, colleges and organizations, citing that it spoils the students and employees. However, if someone knows how to use Facebook well, it can become a platform for engaging new talent and current employees in ways never thought before. Facebook as a platform for recruiting candidates is gaining momentum, but only a handful of people are really using Facebook to find talent.

This book seeks to dispel the myths surrounding Facebook and is an attempt to help patrons to look at Facebook as a means to enhance their online, professional footprint so that they can use this versatile platform to get recruited.

We would like thank some of leading thinkers in the field of education and industry for giving their valuable comments and feedback on this book. I would like to specifically thank Prof. (Dr.) Devendra Pathak, President at Dr. K. N. Modi University, Newai, Rajasthan; and Prof. (Dr.) Ajay Prasher, Dean – Academics and Dean – School of Management, Bahra University for taking time off their hectic duties to provide an unbiased review of this book.

We hope that this book will be a useful guide to youth and others, who would want to know more about using Facebook professionally and get the job of their choice.

Table of Contents

Disclaimer 2
Acknowledgement 3
Chapter 1 - Introduction 5
Chapter 2 – Facebook for Recruitment 8
Chapter 3 – Creating the Ideal Facebook Profile 16
Chapter 4 – Personal Vs Professional Facebook Profile 20
Chapter 5 – Headline and Summary 23
Chapter 6 – Using Facebook to Get Noticed 25
Chapter 7 – Creating Your Facebook Brand 26
Chapter 8 – Tips and Secrets 28
Chapter 9 – Conclusion 31

Chapter 1 - Introduction

There are many ways for you to search for jobs today. As you read through this book, you will find that there are a number of platforms available to you for searching for jobs.

As readers, I know that you would be aware of various platforms for searching for jobs, but my aim was not to highlight the platforms per se, but to let you know that there are a number of platforms are available and you are free to choose the one you think is best for you.

However, the focus of this book will be on how you can use Facebook to search for a job.

The use of social media in recruitment continues to increase in popularity. As people spend more time on these sites, social media savvy organizations will also need to utilize these sites to find candidates. There are a number of reasons why organizations use social media outlets as part of their recruitment strategy. The first, of course, is to source candidates.

Social media recruiting is a cost-effective way to source candidates. Gone are the days of having to pay a premium to advertise in a newspaper and hope that a group of candidates will see the job posting. Now, social media outlets offer "reasonable" pricing for job postings that reach high volumes of active job seekers and, passive candidates. A key benefit to social media recruitment is the ability to reach those workers who are not necessarily looking for a new position. Their social media site activity, however, makes them aware of new job opportunities that might incite them to consider making a change.

Organizations also use social media to target candidates with specific skill sets. They are able to do this through websites of professional or trade associations or by networking through certain social media groups. Over 80% of the positions targeted through social networking are managerial jobs or non-managerial salaried jobs, according to a 2013 SHRM survey.

Today, most individuals are social media savvy. People now spend more time on social networking sites than searching for information. In particular, if an organization is trying to recruit candidates such as recent college graduates, it can find many of them on social networking sites, Facebook being the primary platform. In addition to identifying candidates through social networking sites, organizations are using these resources to screen candidates. They search sites such as LinkedIn and Facebook to glean more information about the candidates, such as their likes, dislikes, the topics they follow, the nature of comments they make on these sites and lastly, recommendations from their professors and colleagues.

Facebook does not need any introduction. Probably, it is one of the most widely recognized companies and services in the world. When I use the word "Facebook," what strikes your mind? Friends, photos, comments, likes, auto-updates – aren't these the words that cross your mind, right now? How about common-interest groups? Would you agree to this? You would definitely be a part of a common-interest group, like a group of your alumni from the college you graduated, or ex-colleagues from your community hostel, or even "Job Seekers."

What I am trying to get to here is that Facebook is not only a tool for individuals to be in touch, but also a platform to link with like-minded people. You may argue that you have LinkedIn, and why Facebook? I will come to this in a few minutes.

Of late, Facebook has ceased to be a social network for connecting with friends only. It's now the world's largest database with 1.35 billion users. As such, Facebook has become a goldmine for recruiters and has been gaining popularity worldwide, as a tool for recruiting and getting to know candidates. "As of March, 2010, Facebook was the second ranked site on the Internet traffic metrics according to alexa.com, accounting for almost 5 percent of all global page views." Today, probably, it is the most frequented website on Internet.

Facebook is a relatively closed network, and can thus make direct sourcing a challenge. Depending on the user's security settings, visitors are allowed limited access, and this makes sourcing on this platform a very big challenge, unlike LinkedIn, which is specifically designed for job search and recruiting candidates. In spite of these challenges, there are ways to generate a pool of excellent candidates, recruit and fill positions using Facebook. Facebook ads offer recruiters a unique opportunity to target Facebook users with job advertisements using keywords, education, location, and even age. Facebook users are provided with detailed information and news about the jobs that are open in these organizations that suit their interests, hobbies, education, and activities. These ads are targeted to the users throughout the day and at staggered times.

With the average Facebook user now spending close to 15 hours and 33 minutes per month on Facebook, Facebook ads can effectively target these users with information that they need, and the cost of targeting is negligible. For e.g. in India, if I were to create a Facebook Ad for a target segment, it would cost me less than $2 per day.

In order to be ahead of the race in recruiting top talent, companies need to look at Facebook as a means of recruitment. Facebook fan page can serve as an alternative to recruiting and sourcing candidates, similar to the company blog or opportunities page, and can directly engage and educate the target users about current and possible future vacancies in the organizations.

With more than 81% of Facebook users outside the US and Canada, Facebook has seen a 41% spurt in active users from Russia, South Korea, Japan, India and Brazil in 2002. 70% of Facebook using job-seekers are male, 63% are under the age of 40 and 40% earn more than $75,000 per annum while 36% are college graduates.

This book is intended for those Facebook users who are keen on seeking a job using Facebook. I will be covering topics like creating an excellent Facebook profile, what are the features of a such a profile, how to create your personal brand and what you need to do in order to be considered actively for current and possible future vacancies in organizations.

To help you create an excellent Facebook Profile, the book begins with an overview of what recruiters look for in a good Facebook profile. I believe that this is an excellent way to start because you will know what recruiters look for, and you can accordingly tailor make your profile to suit their requirements.

While this book is definitely useful for beginners, this will also be useful for people who have been maintaining their profile with Facebook for the past several years.

As you will read through the book, you will also understand that it is important for you to indicate that, even after you have got a job through your strong referral network you value your contacts. Sending thank you notes, and keeping your network engaged are ways in which you can show that you value your contacts.

It takes years to build your network, but seconds to destroy it. Never let this happen to you. If you are in the network to fulfil your self-serving biases, then this is probably not the space for you to be in. You will be wasting your time, as well as those of your network, and it will take no time for the contacts in your network to "Unfriend" you from their list.

With these precautions, I urge you to read this book thoroughly, and put into practice what has been discussed. I am sure it will help you go a long way in achieving your goals and objectives, especially if you are seeking to join a company of your choice.

Chapter 2 – Facebook for Recruitment

When I was pursuing my Master's in Business Administration, I learnt that there are a number of sources for recruiting candidates. Let me take some time to explain these sources, because these sources form the platforms that you will use for searching jobs.

Recruitment is the process that focuses on soliciting resumes from prospective candidates for vacant positions in an organization.

I have been very closely involved in the recruitment process of companies. Whenever I have had to solicit candidates for vacant positions in the organization I worked for, I have resorted to soliciting resumes from prospective candidates. This is in contrast to selection methods; I should rather use the term rejection methods, because once you are shortlisted by the concerned HR department, you are required to go through a series of steps that results in the elimination of unfit candidates from the pool of candidates.

The final step in the rejection process is the actual selection of the candidate(s) who fit into the organizational set up.

With this brief background about the concept of recruitment and selection (rejection), let me proceed to help you understand the platforms that are available for you to search for jobs. These platforms are the same sources that recruiters use for soliciting your resumes.

A number of recruiters and employers tend to use the recruiting yield pyramid to calculate the number of applicants they need to solicit for hiring candidates against the vacant positions in their organization.

Let me help you understand this with the help of an example.

You want to apply to an engineer's position at GE Power in Vietnam, and you find that the employer wants to hire 30 such candidates with experience similar to what you have. You want to be among the 30 candidates to be selected for the vacant positions in the company.

> *Choose a job you love, and you will never have to work a day in your life.* - *Confucius*

So, the recruiter at GE Power in Vietnam makes a small calculation and prepares a pyramid as given below. From experience, the recruiter knows that:

1. The ratio of offers made to actual new hires is 2:1
2. The ratio of candidates interviewed to offers made is 3:2
3. The ratio of candidates invited for interviews to candidates actually interviewed is 4:3
4. Finally, only 1 candidate out of 5 leads generated gets invited for an interview.

The Recruiting Yield Pyramid will now look like this.

Fig. 1: Recruiting Yield Pyramid
Source: Gary Dessler & Biju Varkkey, HRM, 11th Ed., Pg. 179, Pearson Education

So, you see from the above pyramid, if you need to get selected for this position, you have to compete with about 600 candidates, who would have applied from various sources to the company's vacant positions.

How would you want to apply to such a position, which you feel is relevant to you?

You can apply through one of the following methods for various vacant positions in these organizations.

1. Via the Internet, using job portals as well as company websites
2. Through ads placed in newspapers
3. Using Employment and Temp Agencies
4. Executive Recruiters
5. College Recruiters
6. Referrals and Walk-Ins

I know you are well versed in these platforms, and you may be using one or more of them for your job search. My focus is not to explain these platforms, but to give you an idea of how Facebook can also become another platform in addition to the above. Unlike LinkedIn, which has been specifically designed to aid recruiters and has been influencing these methods of recruitment, Facebook is a different ballgame altogether.

Facebook has:
- 936 million daily active users
- 798 million mobile daily active users

LinkedIn has just 414 million users as on 4th Feb, 2016! Hiring managers seeking to hire candidates must look to where candidates spend most of their time to effectively recruit top talent. The modern recruiter has the potential to not only tap into the 259 million users on LinkedIn and 645 million on Twitter, but the 1 billion+ users on Facebook also. In fact, 83 percent of LinkedIn members also use Facebook, and 84 percent of social media users only use Facebook, according to Work4. Sure, these social media sites spoon feed you with loads of information, but what if the perfect hire for a company is on Facebook instead of on LinkedIn? Facebook can be just as fruitful as LinkedIn for recruiting; it's all about employing the right strategies. Yet less than 60% of recruiters use Facebook for recruitment.

Consider these statistics. They will give you an idea of the trends that are pointing fingers at Facebook as the next big thing in recruitment, after LinkedIn.

While Facebook is a relatively closed network, an increasingly large number of people are making their data public, and as such, Facebook presents a goldmine for recruiters. It is not only beneficial for those who employ, but also for jobseekers.

1. An average person spends 1 in every 7 minutes online on Facebook (Work4).
2. 52% of the job seekers used Facebook to look for work in 2012 (Mashable).
3. 22 million people surveyed used social media to find a job in 2012, up from 14.4 million in 2011 (Jobvite Survey).
4. 84% of job seekers have a Facebook profile (Time Business).
5. 50% of users say a brand's Facebook page is more valuable than its website (Work4).
6. 81% of jobseekers want to see job opportunities posted on Facebook career pages (Work4).

How many candidates do recruiters have in their databases? Whatever the number is, it doesn't come close to how many potential candidates are there on Facebook. Facebook provides easy and affordable ways to increase a recruiter's applicant pool. Recruiters can utilize the Facebook Directory to search for users, pages, groups and applications.

Recruiters can post a job for free in the Facebook Marketplace. The ad requires basic information such as location, job category, subcategory, title, why they need to fill this position and the job description and specification. The limitation of a free job posting is that recruiters can't target a specific group of people, which is in contrast to what a Facebook Ad can do.

Facebook Pages pose another free resource for hiring managers to attract potential jobseekers. A Facebook Page is a public profile that enables recruiters to share their business and products with Facebook users. If a company has a Facebook page, recruiters may want to use it as a recruiting tool. And, if the Facebook page is unavailable, they can search for similar pages to find out people who follow these products and services, and then target them. Recruiters need to make sure that the information about their company is relevant and up-to-date. They can also post job openings for their fans to see. Fans are passionate about the company they are following and can be quite passionate about working for this company.

One of the most important options for recruiters using Facebook is to post a Facebook Ad, especially when they are not able to get the results they are seeking through simple searching. The advantage of the ad platform on the Facebook over its rivals – Google AdWords and Yahoo! Advertising is that Facebook Ads have laser targeting ability. With a Facebook Ad, recruiters can choose the exact audience they are seeking to target. The system will ask a series of questions about the characteristics of the people who would want to see a job posting ad. The recruiter will be asked about the group's age, sex and specific keywords related to the position. Facebook will then calculate how many users fit into the criteria posted by the recruiter. Recruiters have the choice to pay per click (how many people clicked on the job ad), pay per impression (how many people potentially saw the ad) and set how much they are willing to pay. Recruiters are also free to decide whether to run the job ad continuously or for a certain time duration only.

Key features of Facebook for recruitment
- Facebook is seen as an important part of the hiring process – close to 50% of employers are using Facebook in their hiring process. A majority (54 percent) of those already using the social networks for hiring anticipate Facebook becoming an integral part of the talent acquisition process in the near future.
- Facebook is cost effective for recruiters – in a recent survey, nearly 90 percent of companies surveyed stated that Facebook has decreased the amount of print advertising needed with regards to their recruiting efforts, making Facebook a cost effective way to find new talent.
- Facebook is a resource for job seekers -- Of the various companies using Facebook to acquire new potential employees, more than half state the importance of networking and referrals. The number one reason (87%) why recruiters prefer to use Facebook is that candidates use Facebook to like their company's Facebook page. This was followed by the fact that they used Facebook as a networking tool.

How to search
The eternal task of finding a job has undergone a couple of huge transformations in the past few years.

Around the turn of the millennium, Craigslist revolutionized job hunting by taking a city's worth of classified sections and condensing them into a single, easy-to-navigate web page.

Now job hunting is undergoing another big shift –into the realm of social media. A new breed of job hunters – call them 'social job seekers' – are utilizing the social networks in ingenious ways to find their dream jobs, and so far they're tasting great success.

It turns out, the more you use a social network, and the more likely you are to find a job through the service: 1 in 4 'super social seekers' successfully network through Facebook, Twitter, or LinkedIn.

This information clarifies how you can search for jobs on Facebook and other social media tools:
- Read Your News Feed
- Get Active in a Group
- "Like" or "Friend" Companies You Want to Work For
- Participate in a Contest.
- Start a Dialogue

The Do's and Don'ts of Facebook when connected to your colleagues:

Having understood why recruiters are turning to Facebook to recruit potential candidates, it is important for you to understand the do's and don'ts when creating your profile. Have patience! I will explain how to create an excellent Facebook Profile later in this book, but before I proceed to explaining, I thought it would be ideal for all of you to understand this first. Once you get a hang of this, it will be easier for you to create an excellent Facebook profile that recruiters will find interesting and have the urge to contact you.

Do's

Stay Professional

Once you start connecting with colleagues, especially on Facebook, it is always better to maintain a professional presence. Of course, you still might want to share those crazy party photos or that TMI story about your child's latest bathroom accomplishment. However, keep them to a minimum.

In order to separate your work network from your personal friends, create Friend Lists. At minimum, create a list with the people you work with and name them – Co-Workers or any other word that you feel is indicative of your professional list. When you share any post on Facebook, you can specify the list to which you want to share this post; in short, what you want others to see or not see is completely in your hands. Post professional stuff to your professional list and personal stuff to your personal list.

Be Active in Groups

Facebook offers you to create groups that can be great for your business. If you can show your boss that you are generating leads through your social networking groups, you might get the green light on be on Facebook for longer duration during work hours. Potentially, these become visible to other companies and you can land the dream job that you have always been seeking.

Update Your Profiles Regularly

Regularly updating your social media profiles is always a good thing, personally and professionally. If your work colleagues see that you are consistently updating your profiles, they won't suspect that an update is preceding a new job search.

Remember: Social Media is Public

Surprise! A connection is not required for your posts to be publicly revealed. While your privacy settings may protect you in some areas, make sure that you have your settings configured properly. Otherwise, people you aren't connected to could end up seeing updates you don't want them to view.

Don'ts

Complain About Your Job

While you may not get fired for complaining about your job on social media, you could create an uncomfortable situation. Complaining about a co-worker could create a strained work relationship going forward. Complaining about a manager could lead to receiving the worst projects and tasks. Complaining about the CEO could mean a minimal to no raise this year. And complaining about your job in general could assure that you won't get that promotion you've been hoping for. Rest assured, if the nature of complaint is really serious, you may even be fired, and getting a new job will be one of the toughest tasks that you will have to face later in life.

Assume Group Activity is Private

Facebook and LinkedIn have detailed privacy descriptions for their public and private groups. Of course, if you post in a secret group today and tomorrow, the owner changes it to an open group, then your comment will be publicly accessible. These privacy policies are especially challenging on Facebook as your friends can see what groups you join and what you post in them, based on their settings. It is better to err on the safer side, than to be sorry later.

Be Obvious About Job Searches

For someone who doesn't update their profiles often, doing a major overhaul can signal the start of a job search to your manager or boss. And it's hard to hide these kinds of changes since Facebook and LinkedIn typically notify your connections about changes. Hence, it's good to regularly update your information.

One trick to try is to create another profile on Facebook, and then review your actual profiles with the fake one. First, review it without connecting with yourself, and then review it after connecting with yourself. This process will give you an idea of exactly what others can see on your profile and in their newsfeed about your activity. Then adjust your actions accordingly!

Finding and following a company on Facebook

Many organizations use Facebook Pages to promote their brands to potential candidates. Not only do they post details about open jobs there, but these pages are often maintained by various members of the recruiting organization.

Before Liking or commenting on these pages, be sure to adhere to the following guidelines:

Post a personal yet professional profile picture. It doesn't have to be the same as your buttoned-up formal picture as no one expects that but it should be of you in a fun and presentable pose.

Visit your "About Me" page and fill it in with as much detail as you can about your education and work history. Be sure to set these elements to Public view.

Begin by Liking the page of your target company or companies.

Next you can then introduce yourself to the community by commenting on and sharing posts. Ensure that the comments and posts are relevant to the owner of the page. Posting jokes and other silly stuff is a strict no-no.

If the page allows, post interesting comments on the owners' timelines that highlight your qualifications.

Of course, don't forget: as you are looking at the company's Facebook pages, in turn, they will probably be looking at your Facebook pages too.

Many new and existing companies are using Facebook to market their products and services to customers affordably and effectively. I am sure you are familiar with

Facebook because you definitely have a personal account, but you may not know all the great ways in which companies market their products and services using Facebook.

Finding Hiring Managers
Let me not get into the specifics of what a company's Facebook page is or how it looks. As a candidate, you are keen to understand who your hiring managers are and how to find them and reach them. The best way to move is to Search Facebook for the company's name and department. You'll be surprised at how many departmental employees and hiring managers you can find on Facebook. You can also use features like Branch Out and Be Known to search for employees and hiring managers from your target company.

Tips to edit Facebook profile for Hiring Managers' Eyes
You can make your Facebook profile visible to people who haven't joined your network yet. If your profile is filled it in completely and thoroughly, then during a job search, nosy hiring managers and recruiters can learn more about you, and contact you at the appropriate time.

Your profile information also helps Facebook to scan and suggest new people to add to your network. The more accurate your profile is the more accurate Facebook's suggestions would be regarding people you can connect with. Make sure your profile is completely filled out, and it is definitely worth the extra five or ten minutes of time you spend to make it complete.

Let us now look at how you can make a professional Facebook profile.

Your profile photo
In Facebook, your profile photo is attached to every post you make and is considered basic information in your privacy settings. The reason is that Facebook is first and foremost a visual platform.

If you're actively seeking employment, use your LinkedIn photo as your Facebook profile image, because you want to give prospective employers the best first impression, and it pays to be as professional as possible. Hence, using your LinkedIn photo as your Facebook profile image makes sense.

Your cover photo
The larger banner behind your profile photo is called your cover photo. This large image can represent anything you like. Think of it like the cover of a book. Pick images from your life that mean something to you, like a nice picture of your family at a wedding, or a beautiful day at the beach where the sunset just took your breath away. Try to keep this photo as simple as possible.

Your "About Me" section
When you click on the Update Info button you find a box called About You that's just waiting for information about you. Your "About You" section should serve a very similar function as your LinkedIn profile summary, in that it communicates who you are professionally and what makes you unique.

The text you enter in this can be set to appear publicly and may be the only prose a hiring manager conducting some preliminary screening may read about you on Facebook.

If you're actively seeking work, consider pasting a copy of your value statement in the About You section of your profile. If you want to add a little more personal information, lead with a professional statement of who you are and conclude with some interests or hobbies.

Work and Education
Be sure your work and education history information matches that of your LinkedIn profile. Hiring managers are looking for inconsistencies (after all, some people lie on their résumés), so if they see that you're consistent with your résumé in several places, they're more likely to believe you.

Favourite Quotations
Sharing who inspires you and what your favourite quotes are can be powerful ways of differentiating yourself. Spend time thinking about your role models and quotes that stick with you.

All the other profile settings
Your Facebook profile also allows you to enter information about the types of music, books, movies, and TV shows you like, as well as your favourite sports teams, activities, and interests. Don't be afraid to fill in this information. Sharing it helps round out your personality in the eyes of a hiring manager.

Just keep in mind that your selections should be appropriate; use the "Would I talk about it in the office?" test to be sure. Revisit these parts of your profile with your career in mind.

Chapter 3 – Creating the Ideal Facebook Profile

With the likes of LinkedIn, and various other online job portals, you may be wondering "Is Facebook the perfect platform for finding jobs?" This can really be an intriguing question to ask in light of the fact that allowing social media platforms like Facebook at work usually drives down productivity to a significant extent. So, when someone says that Facebook can be used to find jobs, it might sound more like an oxymoron. But it has been observed that this social media platform is gaining a lot of relevance when it comes to job search. Today, close to 93% of employers have started using social media for recruitment, and this includes Facebook, Twitter and LinkedIn.

Similar to Talent Solutions service that LinkedIn provides, Facebook also provides various services to employers in order to recruit potential candidates. Facebook has its own job board, competing with LinkedIn's Talent Solutions. I am of the opinion that Facebook will become an excellent platform for recruitment for employers. So, if you are planning to search for a new job, my bet will be on Facebook for this; and I am sure, you will second my thoughts.

But searching a jobs on Facebook isn't just a cakewalk. You need to follow certain steps to get effective results from your job search endeavours on Facebook.

There are three reasons Facebook is so essential when you're looking for a job in today's social media–focused world:

- Most jobs come from referrals. This has been a universal truth, and based on my experience in the HR and recruitment field, I believe that this truth cannot be contested. Most referrals come from friends and family, so it is anybody's guess as to which social network has the highest concentration of friends and family.
- Facebook has more users than the United States has citizens. The number of interconnections, relationships, and interactions between people in the network are infinitely complex. This presents a wonderful opportunity to connect to new people, and thus, give your personal brand a window to reach out to more people. This in turn can accelerate your career.
- You can use Facebook to find out more about a company. Just as firms can get an inside scoop on job candidates by reviewing their Facebook profiles, you can discover the facts about a business by "liking" it's Facebook Page.

> *Pleasure in the job puts perfection in the work.* - Aristotle

Here's a quick look at some of the best ways you can start your job search on Facebook through creating your profile.

Complete Your Profile
This is the first thing you need to do. Most of the users prefer not to take the pain of filling up any field in the form that's not mandatory. But if you are eager to land a job through Facebook, you need to have a complete profile on the platform. Convey to

prospective employers clearly about what you do. This significantly increases the chances of landing a new job through Facebook. It's essential for you to include your professional history in your profile. This is often an area that many people tend to give a miss. I am not trying to blame anybody here, but the very fact that Facebook is seen as a social network for people to connect on a personal front, these fields are generally give a miss. However, you are better off by highlighting your professional information, as this will help you to reach out to employers who seek to recruit candidates through Facebook. Additionally, your complete profile will make you "Google-able," indicating that you are easily searchable on Google. This is something that many employers do look for in potential candidates – ease of being searchable on Google.

Categorize Friends as Professional and Personal
You may have a large number of friends connected on Facebook, but not all of them would be relevant to your job search efforts. Hence, it is imperative for you to categorize your friends on Facebook. You can create a new list, say, "Professional" and bring all those people under this list who you believe would help you in finding your dream job. You may want to share some aspects of your personal life with your professional network, because you would want to have a level of personal touch with your professional contacts. However, when you share your personal stuff, keep it to the bare minimum, and make sure that it is closely related to your job hunt. Do not share a photo with your family on the beach or some casual quote that you would make to an old friend of yours. Remember, keeping it professional with your professional contacts always pays.

Share Content Relevant to Your Job
What do you share on Facebook? Only some humorous pictures and videos? If you are planning to use this social media website for a professional purpose, you need to be selective about sharing as well. You might share a few personal posts with all your friends. But for your professional contacts, make the post relevant to the job profile for which you are planning to apply. You can use some content and share it with your contacts. Make sure to read the content created by other people and comment there. This will also increase your professional engagement on Facebook, which will help significantly in your job search.

Build an Effective Network
No matter what plans you have to go about searching jobs on Facebook, you need to have a network. And the larger your network is, the more help you will get while searching for a new job. Create posts that interest your audience. Engage in conversation with them and let them know your strengths. Besides, you can also request them to let you know about relevant vacancies in their organizations.

Ask Friends for Referrals
Referrals can be a great way to find a job. In fact, job referrals are most effective when you are seeking a change from your current. Share with your network that you are seeking a change, including the type of job and industry you are targeting. If you have a cluster of companies you are targeting and you know people in these companies, you can request them to refer your candidature to these companies (make sure that you are seeking employment in these organizations). Besides, also request them to notify you about requirements elsewhere as well.

Follow Facebook Page of Companies You Want to Work In

I am sure you will not be satisfied with only one company, and you will definitely have a list of organizations you want to target. Ensure that all the companies you want to target have a Facebook page. I believe all companies today have a Facebook page where they share a lot of information – news articles, activities, advertisements, and many others. Ensure that you 'Like' these companies' Facebook pages and follow their activities and posts on a regular basis. This will help you keep abreast of the latest developments in these companies, and groom yourself to join these companies, when the opportunity arises.

Join Groups on Relevant Topics
One way to get heard and seen is to be a member of a group on Facebook. Facebook provides an opportunity for individuals to form groups and become members. Groups can range across a number of topics, and members of a particular group can discuss issues related to the topic. If you are familiar with LinkedIn, these groups in Facebook function in a manner similar to what is seen there. You can also find groups that discuss vacancies in various companies. This will help you to be aware of the requirements and if any of these companies are in your radar, you can start targeting them, providing them with information about what you can do for these companies.

A few years ago, LinkedIn was the only social media platform that was considered to be fit for job seekers. But with time, Facebook is emerging as a major competitor to LinkedIn. With a perfect blend of personal and professional content in your profile, Facebook can be expected to become the most important haunt for job seekers and hiring managers in the near future.

Networking
You can safely assume that most of your colleagues and business partners will be on Facebook. Furthermore, you can also safely assume that recruiters and prospective employers, namely hiring managers, will also be on Facebook. This gives you a unique opportunity to network yourself with whoever is hiring at the present moment.

Status Updates
Whenever you are on a job hunt, make sure that you regularly update your status, with regard to your current situation and what you are looking for in the future. Your network of family, friends, old colleagues, long-time-no-speak acquaintances are all there to help you – this is an inherent aspect of human nature. You should also be cautious with regards to your current colleagues or bosses, for you do not want them to know your latest status updates. You will be delighted to know how much support and help you'll get when you approach your network. Also bear in mind that it is human nature to forget too. By updating your status regularly, you are reminding them of your presence, and providing them with information necessary to help you in your job hunt. This will also help them by recalling you first, as compared to those who weren't in touch with them.

Facebook Marketplace
Craigslist, Gum Tree and other online marketplaces are simple tools that can be very useful in your job hunt. I have a question for you - Have you tried Facebook marketplace? I am sure many of you may not have, while some of you may be aware of what it is, but may not have used, while there may be many of you who many not have heard of this marketplace. I have a task for you now. Go back to your Facebook

profile, and you can browse through your local marketplace for job listings. You will also be able to see a description and the person who posted the job. You can apply directly or contact the person behind the job posting for more information. The catch here is that, Facebook's marketplace may not be as comprehensive as many other marketplaces, such as Craigslist, but you can definitely benefit as there is less likely competition from other roles posted.

Posting ads

Posting your ad is one of the most innovative ways you can use to get noticed on Facebook, though this will cost you. It is very simple to set up an ad campaign on Facebook, and link it to your bio. You can pick the people to whom you want to target and your maximum spend per day (it is a minimum of $1 per day). The more specific you can make the ad, the better it can reach your targeted audience. You want only the right people to click on your ads. If your ad is really innovative and can hit the right vibes with your target audience, you have a fair chance of landing your dream job. While such ads can render targeted audience to evince interest in you, it may or may not lead to your dream job. However, this is certainly another way for you to reach out to your targeted audience.

Integrating your Facebook page with your Facebook profile

If you have a Facebook page and a Facebook personal profile, you can seek to integrate the two. If you visit your profile, you can create your page, and switch between your personal profile and your page.

I am not going to dwell on how you can set up the Facebook page, and how you can switch between the two. This is not the aim of this book, for I only aimed at highlighting the fact that you can integrate your Facebook page and Facebook profile.

However, I believe that you need to understand that your page and profile are separate entities. While your profile is open to public, your profile page is not, unless you decide to make it public.

As mentioned earlier, you can login to your profile, and create pages of your choice and feed it with data that your readers want to see.

You can create a page to focus only on your achievements, the jobs / roles that you have undertaken, and the companies that you have worked in, as well as your educational background and other pertinent information as required by hiring managers.

You can also run specific ads based on the information presented, targeting your prospective hiring managers.

I highly recommend you use Facebook as your Page in the same way you use your personal profile. Comment on posts, connect with other Pages and be social as your Page. Your Page will be much more visible to other Pages and the fans of those Pages.

To cut the long story short, you need to know that your Page and your profile are separate, even though they look connected, and you can navigate between the two when you log into Facebook.

Chapter 4 – Personal Vs Professional Facebook Profile

Most of you use Facebook as a way to interact with friends, post pictures and videos, join groups, and interact with a wide variety of other ways. These characteristics tend to make Facebook the most personal of all the social media sites, and for this reason many of you choose to keep your profiles personal, and I fully second your thoughts. Your Facebook profile is not the best place to be marketing your brand, especially if that brand is you! But that does not mean you cannot go the professional route on Facebook. My recommendation would be to create a page about your company, blog, product, or about yourself. Maintain a page that allows you to maintain a professional image on a personal site. This also allows you to keep your personal profile personal, without mixing it with your professional image. Think about it, you do not want to be Facebook friends with all of your clients and customers! Wouldn't that be an embarrassing situation to be in? Instead, drive them to like your professional page, and market your brand through this page.

How to manage both the profiles
In order to make your profile look professional, you must make a balance between your personal and professional life on Facebook. In the modern times that we live in, the line between our career and our personal life is getting blurred, with any discernible demarcation. So, whatever your profession is, a well ordered Facebook profile will serve to your advantage. Nowadays, many employers and hiring managers even check the profiles of potential employees to get the general idea of what kind of person they are about to hire.

Profile and cover pictures
The first and most important step is to upload some decent profile pictures. While this seems rather easy, it is a very important step. Avoid pictures where you are not visible, or any type of photos which can make you look unreliable or unprofessional. Create a cover photo that identifies you with your passions or a banner of what you love to do. You may be tempted to include a banner of the company you represent, but be very careful when you do this. You

"All our dreams can come true, if we have the courage to pursue them." – Walt Disney

do not want your manager to know that you have included this as your cover photo, and you are out there seeking a job. As an example, if you are a professional photographer, show hiring managers your best photo, so that they are attracted to your page, and want to know more about your portfolio.

Allow people to follow your profile
The follow function allows people to see all of your public updates without being Facebook friends with you. This will help you a lot in getting to know the people with whom you work. What is great about this feature is that anyone who sends you a friend request and you don't accept them, automatically becomes a follower, so you can quickly build a lot of audience with little work.

Public information
When someone visits your profile and he / she is not in your friends list, the person will only see your public information. This section can decide whether someone will follow you, or get interested in the work you do; hence, it is crucial that you write this section with utmost care. Write a convincing and appealing 'About Yourself' description, that states who you are and what you do. Give information about your education, your past jobs and your skills. Potential employers would be interested in understanding more about you, as a person, with such information that you share.

Tell about yourself
As discussed earlier, the line between the professional and personal profiles is very thin. It is desirable that you post your work achievements and include posts about your company. This is a great way to tell the people where you work, who your colleagues are and share your passion with them.

Privacy-Settings
Make sure you do not show anything that may look demeaning to your potential employers. This could include posts, photos and any other stuff that you may like or share with others. In general, if you have a page to showcase your Knowledge, Skills and Attitudes (KSA), then you need not worry about specific privacy settings, because you are the admin of the page, having complete control. You can thus, decide to invite people who can see your page.

On the other hand, if you are sharing your personal profile to professional contacts, or you do not have a specific page, then you need to be extra careful, especially about the posts, photos or other stuff that you like or share. Potential employers and hiring managers would be interested to know more about your personal life too, and wouldn't be too happy to see you share information that they feel is not fit for their organization.

Distinguish between personal and professional profiles

Know how you want to be perceived in general
Most people immediately jump to the conclusion that separate is better, and in a lot of cases it is. However, it's worth keeping in mind that your personal life can sometimes benefit your professional life. People are going to want to see that you're a real human and not just words on a computer screen. Part of helping your articles pop or your social accounts thrive professionally is actually bringing in a little bit of your personality and personal life. With this in mind, you can start to define what you want these two brands to mean to you. Where do you want them to intersect? How are you going to use one to help the other? Once you know how you want to be perceived, you can begin taking appropriate steps to make it happen.

Know which social account to use when posting content
This is definitely what many people think of when they want to post any content, and rightfully so. Posting on social media is going to be the biggest challenge when trying to keep your personal and professional usage separate. The most significant thing you can do is know which social platform to use at which time. In other words, think about the content you want to post and then decide which account suits it best. Though this is a

pretty obvious choice, I felt it would be worth mentioning it here because you 'do have to know who your audience is.'

Decide who you should allow as "friends" on each social network
This is arguably the most crucial point that you need to consider. Determine which social account you want to be primarily professional and which one is going to be primarily personal, so that you know who to connect with on each. This will help you know what content to publish where.

The other accounts, on the other hand, are completely up to you. Many people choose to keep Facebook personal and not accept friend requests from anyone at work or in the industry, but it doesn't have to be that way. Some people set up two separate Facebook accounts altogether. You get to choose what you want; so, choose wisely.

Focus on privacy
Another important aspect that you cannot forget is about your privacy. If you have your Facebook account strictly to share with your friends on a personal note, then set your privacy to 'Private,' so that only your friends can see your content. This way, you can be sure that your professional contacts do not get to see what you post as part of your personal network.

Again, as mentioned earlier, it is you who has to decide your privacy levels, and act accordingly.

Google yourself every once in a while
How would you know what others are posting about you in their blogs or other media? While you may have diligently set up your privacy according to your audience for all your profiles, you can't stop people from writing something about you online and publishing it. In such cases, the best thing for you to do is to do a quick Google search about yourself. You can also set up Google Alerts to alert you about possibilities of your name being published without your knowledge.

Whether the publicity is good or bad, it is something for you to decide – if you believe it leads to a backlash regarding something you did or write in the past, it is definitely bad; I mean the backlash. What if the post you made in the past was only your opinion and you only wanted to share your thoughts, in a very neutral tone? And someone has made a very nasty comment based on what you have written. While you definitely need to know that such a comment is made against you, you will also need to take appropriate action.

More often than not, the ones publishing posts about you are the ones you know. The idea here is to ensure that you are in control of your profile, and if you aren't sure, try searching yourself online, because you may never know what is amiss and what actions you need to take.

The name of the game here is keeping the brands separate, not blending them together. If someone posted something personal about you on his/her blog that you don't like, it's simply your job to know about it, and then ask that person to make it private or use your nickname instead of your real name.

Chapter 5 – Headline and Summary

You have now answered questions like – "What is your job target?" "Who are you?" and "What do you want?" You are now ready to move ahead. The next step is to determine which headline fits your unique situation. Remember "stating which type of job seeker you are will help the employer understand your motivations"? The reason for using a headline is to let your potential hiring manager understand your motivations up front.

Objective
Typically, the objective statement is designed to tell the employer what you want, but ends up saying very little, if anything, about what you will contribute. This is the reason why so many career experts tell you not to provide one and recommend you to use a "Title" instead.

There are varying opinions on whether it is good to use an objective statement. While some articles claim objectives are useless, others claim that they are a necessity in your profile. What others say or claim is none of my botheration, for what I believe is that, if written correctly, objectives are a great way to inform others what you really want to do.

Objectives, it has been observed, is more useful for someone with little or no work experience – a freshman to be precise. An additional point worth considering is Your Summary Statement. A summary statement gives potential employers an overview of your strengths. The summary statement can also be standalone or in conjunction with your Objective. Generally speaking, for people with experience, an objective may not really make sense, and the summary would suffice.

> *"Opportunities don't often come along. So, when they do, you have to grab them."* – *Audrey Hepburn*

Here are a few examples of bad and good objective statements;

Bad Examples:
- *Objective 1:* Obtain a full-time job with your company to learn new skills.
- *Objective 2:* Payroll, AP/AR, filing, typing, answering phones and greeting people
- *Objective 3:* Obtain part-time work in a challenging and rewarding environment

Good Examples:
- *Objective 1:* New to the workforce with a recent Payroll and Office Administration certificate. I am eager to perform various payroll and AP/AR duties, as well as provide General Office support.
- *Objective 2:* Secure a full-time Office Administration position, where my contributions include; more than 5 years' experience performing various payroll and AP/AR duties and providing General Office Support.
- *Objective 3:* Skilled Administrative professional seeking new career path within Project Management. I am able to immediately contribute advanced knowledge of MS Project and have demonstrated experience with allocating resources and scheduling project details.

Summary or Highlights of Qualifications
Summary statements are most often a series of statements highlighted behind bullet points that describe your skills and strengths through the use of action verbs. These can be very effective if what you say in each statement is reflected somewhere in the body of your resume. However, avoid empty statements.

What is an empty statement? Statements that do not identify skills that are transferred to your job. Example would be "hard-working, friendly, reliable, dependable and punctual." The above does not really tell me whether you have transferred them to your job. Is there any backing that you can do with these traits? Probably no! and my advice is to leave them off your profile – both in your resume as well as Facebook profile. It is another distractor and your prospective employer may just trash your profile and never want to consider it at all.

Use a summary statement that answers these questions; "what is your job target, who are you, what do you want and what type of job seeker are you?" A well-crafted profile statement will provide this information in 3-4 sentences. Use your Facebook Page or Professional Profile that you created for searching jobs.

As with your resume, the key to an effective profile statement is to be specific but brief, relevant to the position you're applying for and most importantly, to show your motivation. Motivation is a direct reflection of your passion, commitment, and desire for your chosen profession and/or position. By providing your motivation up-front, chances are, your next employer has found value in your ability to be open and will likely continue reading for more information about your background. Below are two examples of good profile statements:
- Profile 1: Events Coordinator with more than 10 years' experience seeking a full-time, permanent position that requires a self-starter with passion for working with diverse populations. My background includes planning, coordinating and producing small and large-scale events. I bring maturity, tact and enthusiasm to contribute within a thriving team environment and possess excellent interpersonal and negotiation skills to facilitate various services and contract details.
- Profile 2: Registered Nurse with passion for providing quality health care services for children within hospital and private practice settings. My focus is on promoting excellent patient care with a compassionate and empathetic approach. Committed to continuous education, ongoing training and professional growth opportunities that incorporate my background and experience toward a career in Pediatrics.

Chapter 6 – Using Facebook to Get Noticed

Facebook is a social networking tool that can be vital in helping you land a new job; especially when you can modify your profiles to appeal to potential employers, and use the websites mainly for professional connections and correspondence. Using Facebook can connect you with multiple business contacts in your local area and around the world, and can also help you attract the attention of employers who are specifically searching for candidates with your expertise. Although Facebook's layout is primarily designed to connect you with people on a personal level, you can manipulate your profile to convey a professional persona; whereas with LinkedIn, the platform is already designed to connect you with contacts in a professional manner.

Methods of finding a new job by using Facebook
- Log into or create your Facebook profile. You will be required to log in using your email address and password, or sign up to create a new profile.
- Create or modify your Facebook profile to convey a professional tone and manner. Since your profile will be viewed by business professionals and other important contacts, you will need to display information that supports your professional reputation. Indicate professional interests and hobbies in your profile instead of personal interests. For example, if you work in computer programming, and enjoy developing computer games and applications, indicate this interest in your profile.
- Network with professional contacts. Connecting with professional users and businesses can help get your Facebook profile noticed by a number of potential employers or referring users. Search for business contacts by email address or name, then send each contact a Facebook friend request so you can establish a connection.
- Join the Facebook groups of businesses and employers you want to work for. The Facebook pages for businesses and companies will allow you to join discussions and conversations related to those businesses, and will keep you updated on company news and other events. Visit the Facebook page of the company or business that interests you, then select the "Like" button to become involved with and join that particular Facebook group.
- Develop a Facebook page that showcases your professional background and abilities. You can then use your Facebook page to publish information about your skills, experience, and job search.
- Publish status updates that state you are looking for a new job. Your status updates will appear in the timeline of other Facebook users who are on your Friends list, or in the timeline of those who subscribe to your Facebook page.

Chapter 7 – Creating Your Facebook Brand

If you're looking for a job, your online profile is more important to you now than ever before!

Being in the job market can sometimes be a little soul-destroying, with many advertised jobs getting far more applications than before. The job boards are still working for many job seekers, but in the age of Web 2.0, there are plenty of other things you can do to stand out from the crowd and get that position you want.

So how can you successfully market yourself online and really stand out?

Follow these 10 easy tips and watch your personal online brand come alive!

Facebook Business Page

Get private—if only temporarily
Make sure your privacy settings are set to Friends only, at least for the time you're in the job market. You don't want your friends sharing personal pictures with the rest of the world.

Use a Facebook business page
Set up a Facebook page to display your professional side. The beauty of a Facebook page is that it's searchable via Google, so when a prospective employer is checking you out, your Facebook page should rank high in the search terms because Facebook pages are quickly indexed.

Use your Facebook business page as a blog
Add to your business page plenty of information, not only about yourself, but also write posts in the Notes tab about your thoughts and opinions of your industry. For example, if you're a marketer, maybe write about how you would approach a particular brand's campaign, or what you think worked or didn't work about a campaign. Use the Notes tab as a way of blogging. You can add photos of work you've completed or any recent marketing projects you managed.

Promote your page to spread through your friends
Use this Facebook business page just as you would any other business page. Add value and information, get people to "Like" it, and promote it.

Use Facebook Ads
Consider making use of Facebook Ads. For a couple of dollars' a day, you can write a nifty ad stating that you're looking for a position in your chosen field. If you're in marketing, this should give you free rein to write a creative ad to promote yourself. Facebook Ads can be targeted to show up only on members' pages in a particular city, along with a whole lot of other targeting criteria.

> *Your work is to discover your work and then with all your heart to give yourself to it. - Buddha*

Measure and tweak
Measure your ad's effectiveness every few days with campaign statistics, and tweak it where necessary. Don't simply stick with your first ad attempt; you may get better results with something completely different.

What does your professional headline say about you?
Does your professional headline say exactly what you do—the real essence—or does it say "Manager at ABC Ltd."? You have 120 characters, so be creative. Try something like "I help manufacture and distribute the tastiest chocolate in the USA."

Use your HOT LINKS
Have you used your hot links appropriately? Rather than using the standard "my website," choose the "other" option and create a link back to your Facebook business page or your blog. Think about exposure of your own personal brand while you're in the job market.

List yourself in a group job section
Anyone can advertise their job vacancies in any of the groups they belong to, but why not do it the other way around? Why not post an ad in the jobs section of the groups you're a member of, stating what position you're looking for?

Promote your online brand
Add your network links to your email signature. That way, the person receiving your application will get the correct profile if they do decide to check you out, so make it easy. You want them to see your great personal brand.

Working on managing an effective online profile, whether there is something unsavoury out there about you or not, can only be a positive thing. It takes a little time and effort, but the results are worth the efforts that you put in.

If you do find someone online with the same name as you, but with an appalling online image, you may want to mention that to the interviewer or business connection up front. "Don't confuse me with XYZ who has a bad trading record with eBay."

Never stop working at your online profile, write articles for online sites in your industry and blog posts if you blog, and find some way to keep your name at the top of the list!

Chapter 8 – Tips and Secrets

Social-networking sites are putting printers of business cards out of business. Instead of trading a small piece of paper, people are now trading names and tracking one another down on sites such as LinkedIn and Facebook.

While LinkedIn has a decidedly professional bent, Facebook can be a much more intimate look into one's personal life and inner circle of friends. Still, a lot of folks are on Facebook and use it as a professional networking tool. But is it right for you?

As Facebook makes it easy to blur the lines between the professional and personal aspects of your life, most experts urge caution, unless, perhaps, you work in the entertainment industry.

Here are the Seven tips to put your best face forward on Facebook:

Tip 1: Keep It Strictly Professional
"Have a consistent message," meaning if you're marketing yourself as a top accountant, make sure your Facebook profile reflects that image. You can keep your business contacts and personal friends separate on Facebook with appropriate apps. If it is not possible, then have separate profiles for your personal and professional contacts.

Tip 2: Mind Your Status
You can use your status to let people know about additional projects you're working on, which sends a message that you're more than just what you do at work every day. Mind you, if your coworker is also your friend on Facebook, make sure you do not accidentally throw yourself under the bus by revealing you weren't really sick when you called in sick to work.

Tip 3: Choose Your Friends and Groups Carefully
The people you make friends with and the groups you join are a reflection of who you are. Think through the requests you accept and the company you keep on Facebook, because potential employers may take these into account very seriously. One group of Virgin Atlantic employees started a Facebook group in which they openly traded insults and complaints about customers and colleagues -- and 13 of those workers were fired. If you're an employee, you have to be considered an advocate of your employer at all times.

> *Success is how high you bounce when you hit bottom. - General George Patton*

Tip 4: Mind Your Identity
Another plus of keeping your privacy settings high or, ideally, keeping your profile strictly professional, is that you're less likely to divulge personal information that could leave you at risk of identity theft. The personal email account of former Alaska Governor Sarah Palin was famously hacked by someone who successfully guessed the answers to her security questions. Avoid divulging your pets' names, your mom's maiden name and other details that could leave you vulnerable to fraud by including only professional details on any social-networking site.

Tip 5: Don't Get Sucked In
It's been raining that entrepreneurs are getting a lot of encouragement to be on Facebook and they're marketing with full force on Facebook. "But it's not the be-all, end-all solution for marketing. It may have some value toward your bottom line, but it may not if you're spending too much time on it. Check your return on investment."

As recruiters and companies look to Facebook as an additional source of finding new talent, it is important that you are at least familiar with such sites. "In terms of new partnerships and for job search purposes, it can be a great networking tool to let people know about you, and it's a great way to learn about people and companies and options. Just be sure to use these sites in a savvy manner to your benefit.

Tip 6: Classify your friends
You have the option of creating new lists, with your existing friends. You can create lists like Professional or Work, and include all those with whom you would want to have a strictly professional relationship. Doing so can help you target your work related status updates appropriately, and avoid getting caught at the wrong place and wrong time.

Tip 7: Post content and respond to other people's postings.
For your professional contacts, post updates about your and your company's achievements. Make sure you include related news from all possible sources. Additionally, make sure you pay attention to your professional group's postings. Small actions like "Liking" their posts and posting meaning and insightful comments will help you find newer avenues. On Facebook, things get reciprocated, and when you put up a post, it is likely that many of your professional contacts will find a way to "Like" and "Comment" meaningfully on those posts.

Some Secrets that I would like to Share

Conduct a people search instead of a job search
While a number of jobs are posted online, most hiring managers prefer to get referrals from their employees and most times, vacancies are filled without posting details of the job. It is noted that more than 80% of vacancies are filled through networking, but very few have sought to use social networking sites to search for one. Use the 3-step search approach as given below to get the job you want.

The 3-step people search:
1. Identify the top five companies that you would like to work for: Use a focused approach instead of flooding thousands of inboxes with spam. You want to brand yourself, not only as the best fit person for a job, but also as someone who is eager and ecstatic to work for the company.
2. Use search engines to track employees that currently work there: There are over 130 million blogs on various websites and you can search through them to possibly find someone who works at one of your top five companies. You can also search through corporate groups, pages and people on Facebook, Twitter and possibly LinkedIn too. Finally, there are people search engines such as pipl, peek you, and wink, you can rely upon. Once you find a contact name, try googling it to see if there is any additional information about that person.

3. Connect with the person directly: Social media has broken down barriers, to a point where you can message someone you aren't friends with, without any hassles. Before you message a target employee, realize that they receive messages from people asking for jobs all the time and that they might not want to be bothered on Facebook, where their true friends are. As long as you've done your homework on the company and them, tailor a message that states who you are and your interest, without asking for a job at first. Get to know them and then by the 3rd or 4th messages, ask if there is an available opportunity. You can also try getting an intro to the person through common friends, if you have any.

Use attraction-based marketing to get job offers
The traditional way of searching for a job was proactive, forcing you to start a job that you might not have enjoyed. The new approach is about building a powerful personal brand and attracting job opportunities directly into your doorstep. Wouldn't this be interesting? How do you do this? Become a content producer instead of just a consumer; and the best way to do this is to launch a blog that centers around your expertise and passions.

Your passion and commitment to writing, being creative and consistent will help you in the long run. Blogs are non-intrusive, harmless and a very generous way of getting recruiters interested in your brand. You can get a job without even asking for it. Recruiters will definitely fall in love with your blogs, and you, and send you opportunities related to your blog. Hence, both you and your recruiter will become happy in the end.

There are a number of ways in which you can start blogs and be creative. WordPress is excellent for beginners or choose GoDaddy or Bluehost to host WordPress blogs on your website.

Advertise your brand using Facebook Social Ads
Facebook Social Ads allow businesses and individuals to advertise using Facebook's news feed. This program works similar to Google's AdSense but you can use a picture and it's more "word-of-mouth friendly" because ads travel through the news feed of your friends.

I don't want to explain how to create an ad. However, I would like to highlight three important aspects that you need to remember while creating an ad.
- Title. What is the ad for? The title is the most important piece of your ad because it has the most "text" emphasis. Be creative and try to be as specific as you can.
- Picture. Use a picture that is professional, yet personal in nature, to give your prospective ad reader an idea of who you are.
- Description. Don't write your resume, but instead give the viewer a quick description of who you are, what you do and what you want in as few words as possible.

Once you create your ad, either link it to your Facebook page, LinkedIn profile or blog/website. These ads are all about targeting a specific group that would care about your resume or hiring you for that matter. Keep in mind your major target audience, company and location.

Chapter 9 – Conclusion

Can you really get a job with Facebook? Well, let's just say it's not going to overtake LinkedIn anytime soon on that front. But if you are really spending time on Facebook, why not turn it into something productive. Add it to your social media job searching strategy along with LinkedIn, Twitter and any other platform that you use. Another weapon in your job hunting arsenal is not going to hurt.

Facebook can be a secret weapon for those looking for jobs. And not just by posting: "Hey, I'm looking for a job." Such posts on Facebook can also harm your prospective job search. Recruiters will definitely visit your Facebook profile and judge you, based on what you have posted.

Use Facebook to get noticed by the companies you want to work for. "Facebook offers you numerous ways to engage with your target companies. You can Like pages, participate in discussion groups and do a variety of things to get noticed by your target company."

When people are looking for a job on Facebook, a lot of times they quickly set all of their Facebook settings to 'private.' It is always a good idea to have a closer look at Facebook's latest privacy features.

Instead of hiding everything, you can make you work and education information public. If recruiters don't know where you work, they can't call you for a job opportunity. The idea here is to share the information you want people to find.

Check what your Facebook profile looks like to the public. You'll need to be logged into Facebook with an account that isn't a friend. Search for your name and poke around your profile. Scrub anything you don't want to show the world.

Facebook allows users to get to know your business more intimately. You can communicate through status updates, photos, messages and more. The key to being successful with Facebook is interaction. If patrons post a question on your page, respond! The more you respond and interact with the people who "Like" your page, the more they will talk about your business to others and share your page, getting you more "Likes." Of course, interaction isn't the only thing that will get you noticed. You have to tell your followers what is going on with your business: update them with statuses, photos, links and more. If you provide useful information to your followers, it will make them want to engage with you more. For those unfamiliar, it might be overwhelming at first to start up a Facebook page.

Facebook is a primary vehicle of communication today, and because much of that communication is public, it's no surprise some recruiters and hiring managers are tuning in to realize the power Facebook could bring to their recruiting efforts.

www.ingramcontent.com/pod-product-compliance
Lightning Source LLC
Chambersburg PA
CBHW040820200526
45159CB00024B/3058